C000149972

HOCKEY UMPIRING

Published by

Sports Resources

Devon, England

Published by:

Sports Resources Ltd

1 Hawkmoor Cottages

Bovey Tracey, Devon, TQ13 9NJ, England

info@sportsresources.co.uk

www.sportsresources.co.uk

First published August 2001 (A Guide to Umpiring Hockey)

8th edition published December 2012 (Hockey Umpiring)

ISBN: 978-0-9541169-8-9

Design and artwork by VJ Design. www.vjdesign.co.uk

Front cover photograph : Frances Block, GB umpire at the London 2012 Olympics, courtesy of Peter Savage ©.

www.hockeyimages.co.uk

Other photographs Jane Hodgson, EHB, Wolfgang Sternberger (FIH) ©.

CONTENTS

ACKNOWLEDGEMENTS

I make special mention of the many umpires ranging from those who officiate at club level through to those whose talent has taken them on to the international World Panels. Thank you to all for your valuable contributions.

In addition, I thank friends, colleagues, players, umpires managers and coaches who have willingly offered their time and input; VJ Design, design and artwork; the photographers and all of the umpires and players who feature in the photographs – thank you.

Jane Nockolds

FIH Umpires Manager and Coach

World Panel Hockey Umpire (retired)

INTRODUCTION

This is a book for all hockey umpires; for those who are young or new to umpiring through to those who are measured as close to reaching their potential.

The aim of *Hockey Umpiring* is to provide umpires with advice, guidance and a variety of valuable facts and tips all of which when considered together will lead to better performance and greater enjoyment. The content has been gathered from umpires, coaches, players and managers operating at all levels of the sport - from local club hockey to the FIH World Panel.

In the pages that follow we will consider the Rules, the necessity for full understanding of the play, tactical awareness, the skills of the umpire, the need for good communication, physical and mental fitness and the language of the umpire, including body language and how to speak through your whistle. We will look at areas that sometimes cause confusion, the importance of developing confidence and coping with conflict.

Hockey is changing. It is getting ever faster. The skills are less mechanical; the variation of pass and technique so competently executed on the international stage are now in 2012, commonly demonstrated at junior and club level.

It is a growing sport. The worldwide audience created through increasing levels of television exposure and the development of internet viewing has contributed immensely to the development of the game. There is less whistle, more flow, less interference, more management, less boredom, more excitement for the audience and the participants...and the umpires have a genuinely big role to play.

Chapter 1

THE ESSENTIALS

Assessing Yourself

Even if you are a regular umpire it's worth stopping every once in a while and thinking about where you have come from and where you want to go. If you are a new or inexperienced umpire, you will benefit by giving some thought to your past – your 'service history' so as to identify your potential strengths and possible weaknesses.

1	Have you umpired before?	Yes	No
2	Have you read the Hockey Rules book?	Yes	No
3	Do you have all of the umpiring equipment?	Yes	No
4	Do you have a good technical understanding?	Yes	No
5	Are you aware of the tactics of play?	Yes	No
6	Are you physically fit?	Yes	No
7	Can you run and sprint?	Yes	No
8	Can you run backwards and sideways?	Yes	No
9	Are you a good communicator?	Yes	No
10	Are you fair and honest?	Yes	No
11	Are you able to manage conflict?	Yes	No
12	Is your eye-sight very good?	Yes	No

The players will always say that you are only as good as your last game. Have a think about it…How good was your last game and what went well? What could have been better? Why did things work or not work? Was it your fault? Did you seek feedback? Did you self assess? Did you feel comfortable and confident during the game? Did it show? Did you really give it 100%?

1	Did you arrive with plenty of time to spare?	Yes	No
2	Did you feel that you had prepared well?	Yes	No
3	Did you have a pre-match chat?	Yes	No
4	Did you umpire as per the pre-match chat?	Yes	No
5	Did you operate as a team from start to end?	Yes	No
6	Were you fair and honest at all times?	Yes	No
7	Were your decisions good?	Yes	No
8	Were your decisions consistent?	Yes	No
9	Did you use your management skills well?	Yes	No
10	Did you communicate effectively?	Yes	No
11	Do you think you looked competent?	Yes	No
12	Were you conscious of your body language?	Yes	No

Preparation

Good preparation is made up of a number of components. Some are physical, some are mental. Some are brought on by the self; some are brought on by a colleague or a situation. Some are good fortune and some are coincidental. The key is to recognise the importance of preparing well and to be accountable for it…take responsibility and don't risk regretting your performance. "If you fail to plan, you plan to fail". Most of us know this proverb and will have considered it at some stage either at home, within our leisure activity or in the workplace.

A good example of mental preparation is self-talk. Before you go on to a hockey pitch there should be one very clear thought at the front of your mind… "I am going to do my best to umpire better than I ever have before." It may sound silly, but actually it's a common thought, particularly from the more experienced umpires.

Self talk can enhance focus, confidence and self-esteem. Thoughts have a profound impact on actions. For an umpire

7

to use positive self-talk and to be motivated, to think optimistically before each game, to encourage him or herself to be at their best and fully concentrated is an important part of preparation and it can significantly contribute to a higher level of performance, success and enjoyment.

However, we all know that it isn't just thinking (self-talk) that allows us to go out and umpire well, particularly for umpires who have less experience or are completely new to the role. For you there are a number of other factors that need to be in place.

Here are some suggestions to help you before you go out to umpire your first match.

1 Read about umpiring

If you are or were a player, you will have an understanding of the rules of hockey and be able to recognise the reason for a penalty. However, it's different when you are an umpire. You need to think about applying the rules and understanding them not as pages in a book, but as what actually happens in front of you – on the pitch. In addition to reading this book, you will benefit from reading the umpiring section of the FIH Hockey Rules book.

2 Watch Hockey

Don't go to a game or watch it on the TV or internet purely to view and consider the play. It is important and key to your learning to watch the umpires and the umpiring. See how they apply the rules and control the match.

Before the game they will meet and during this time they will discuss how they will operate consistently and as a team. Responsibilities, consistency, management and control will be important to them. They will arrange and confirm cooperation techniques and plan how to communicate effectively throughout the match.

They will check the pitch together, ensuring that it is correctly marked, that the goal posts are placed immediately behind the back-lines and that the nets are firmly attached to the posts and the cross-bar, so there can be no doubt when the ball has entered the goal. They also decide who will time each half and which side of the pitch they will take. The normal playing time is 70 minutes, each half being 35 minutes in length. Half time is normally 5 or 10 minutes.

TIP It's a good idea to carry a supply of string or adhesive tape (insulating tape is perfect for the job) and a pair of blunt nosed scissors so that you can repair or secure damaged or loose-fitting nets before the match begins. Although this responsibility primarily rests with the home team, evidence suggests that they rarely have the equipment to deal with it. Do them a favour and be equipped to handle it! All you need do is pass them the tool-kit and ask them to get on with it!

When the match begins – watch the umpire on your side of the pitch. Notice how they move almost continually (not unnecessarily but in accordance with the demands of the play), especially when the ball is in or approaching their half of the pitch.

Look at where the umpire stands for set-pieces. These include free-hits, hit-ins, hit-outs, penalty corners, corners and penalty strokes. Are they suitably ahead of the play? Do they have an angle that allows them to see as much as possible?

Notice the umpire's signals. They should always be clear and given with confidence. Are they?

Initially you may recognise only some of the offences. You will certainly not see everything, but gradually the picture will become clearer and you will recognise more and apply the penalties appropriately when you start umpiring.

3 Two things you can practice at any time

Signalling is the first. This is best practised in front of a mirror! You may find that what you believe you are doing is not what you see in your mirror, and that is exactly what the players would see. Could they be confused by your signals? Do you look confident? Try to get your signals right before you go out to umpire.

The second is how you blow your whistle. Does it have tone? Does it send clear messages? Will the players know when an offence was minor but requiring a stoppage or a penalty, versus the more serious offence…the big whistle, the strong whistle.

TIP Experiment with your technique. It's important to be able to speak with your whistle. You need to learn to vary the tone. When a serious offence occurs, you will need to blow the whistle strongly. This is often referred to as a blast. When a minor offence occurs, a quieter whistle is preferred... just a beep to stop the play and award the penalty. One of the best ways to practice without raising a few eyebrows is to pretend there's a problem with your whistle before the game starts and repeatedly blow it and practice tone variation, or better still, buy a dog and use a whistle to train it!

TIP Remember that you must appear confident. Make a big effort to sell yourself and your decisions. A slow or hesitant signal or whistle indicates uncertainty. Try to avoid it.

4 Umpiring Clothing

Most hockey teams have an attractive team kit. They look smart and are readily identifiable. Umpires should also look smart and have distinctive kit. It's important that the players can quickly distinguish the umpires. They don't want or have time to search for you or lose sight of you. You must avoid merging into the spectators in the background or other players on the pitch. Wear shirts of the same colour and dark coloured (ideally black) trousers or skirt (ladies note, a skirt is not compulsory!) and footwear suitable for the playing surface.

5 Equipment

The equipment you need includes a copy of the current Hockey Rules book, two whistles (one a spare), a stop-watch, a set of coloured hockey warning cards, a coin for the toss, a pen or pencil, and a match score pad for recording the score and the number of any player receiving an official warning (i.e. a card or cards).

6 Get to know umpires

Someone in your club who is interested in your progress will be able to help you. In addition, most counties, regions or states have a hockey umpiring administrator or secretary and a number of umpire coaches. There are regular events for umpires in most areas. These include lectures, presentations and coaching days and evenings. The benefits of attending these events go beyond extending your umpiring knowledge and skills – you find yourself in a social environment, among new friends and colleagues and inevitably, new opportunities will become available to you.

TIP Take responsibility. Go out there and find out what's available to you and get involved. Every opportunity to learn a little bit more should be taken.

Chapter 2

PSYCHOLOGICAL SKILLS

Some players and coaches and occasionally spectators, suggest that umpires think and behave like robots. There are occasions when we might look a little robotic but it's usually down to nerves or failure to recognise a player's intentions and subsequently making the wrong decision or no decision. In truth, umpires are no more like robots than players and very importantly, umpires face emotion and pressure. Sometimes it can be tough out there!

However, taking the time and making the effort to understand and develop your psychological skills will enhance your performance and the better you do, the more you will relax and the more confident and competent you will become. Nine times out of ten, umpires who have and 'deliver' these psychological skills will be those that perform at the higher levels of the game and get the most pleasure, the most reward from the game.

Psychological skills include relaxation, imagery, communication, confidence and setting personal goals.

Relaxation

Being suitably relaxed and free from anxiety before and during a match is crucial to achieving your potential. It doesn't matter what level of hockey you are umpiring – whether it's the world cup final or a local cup game, in all cases there is pressure to perform. Sometimes you put this pressure on yourself and sometimes other people put it on you.

The critical attribute of a successful umpire is to remain calm and in control despite adverse conditions. The best umpires are distinguished by their ability to make good and correct decisions and take control of the game under pressure. They don't get stressed or if they do, it isn't visible. They look calm and relaxed and seem to be enjoying the challenges confronting them.

What are the potential sources of stress that are unique to the official or umpire?

> The fear of failure
> The fear of inadequacy
> Perceived loss of control

Fear of failure is 'the number one' and in its most basic form, this can include the fear of having a bad game, worrying about getting a poor evaluation from a coach, watcher or assessor or not meeting your own expectations.

Fear of inadequacy can be based on real or imagined incompetence or lack of physical or psychological preparation.

Perceived loss of control is associated with a feeling of being ineffective. Some umpires feel a loss of control immediately they are challenged or criticised by a coach or player/s. This is a real problem and the stress that comes as a result usually leads to a 'less than best' performance.

So how can you make yourself relax before a match and what can you do to reduce any anxiety levels you might have? There are physical relaxation techniques and there are mental relaxation techniques. The physical techniques include breath control and progressive relaxation (muscle relaxation) and the mental techniques include self-talk and thought stopping. A number of publications detail these techniques and there is also a wealth of information on the web.

> **TIP** If you are nervous or stressed, try tensing and relaxing specific muscles as a part of your preparation. Tension and relaxation are mutually exclusive – it's impossible to be relaxed and tense at the same time.

> **TIP** When you think, you talk to yourself. Self talk is great because it can (assuming it's positive) enhance your self esteem, confidence and focus and it reduces your self-doubt and anxiety. Most of us do it during a match without realising it. If we made ourselves do it as a part of our preparation we would surprise ourselves at the level of difference it can make.

If you are like most new umpires you probably aren't really in touch with your self-talk and neither do you realise the powerful impact it's having on your performance. My recommendation is that you gather some more information and see what a positive impact it can have. It has a big role to play in developing your confidence and therefore allowing you to be more relaxed and less anxious.

Imagery

Imagery involves you visualising yourself doing things well. It's about creating positive images in your mind – like being in the right place to see clearly and make that split second decision with precision and accuracy, about looking confident and focused, about seeing yourself enjoying the experience and doing it well.

Umpires can use imagery to overcome barriers. It may be that you have had a bad experience with a team or player or with another umpire – someone who intimidated you or didn't assist you when you needed it and therefore put you under pressure. Try to visualise yourself dealing with the person or the situation well. Visualise yourself as being strong, poised, calm, assertive… it really does help you in your preparation.

Communication

Good communication is crucial to your success as an umpire and it isn't something that starts when you first blow the whistle. Neither is it something that stops when the game is over. Communication starts from the moment you arrive at the club or at the event. Sometimes it can be before that e.g. in a telephone call or an e-mail to the club manager or captain or the local administrator who organised your appointment to the game. When does it stop? One could suggest it doesn't! It certainly should continue into the post-game activity. This could mean the clubhouse or the bar or even in a discussion at a later time.

It is also very important that you recognise that it's not just about how or what you say or write, but also and arguably more importantly, it's about how you look…your **body language.**

The way you stand, your movements, your gestures and your expression are all key contributors. Communication is about how we send and receive messages and our body language is a very strong messaging agent!

Confidence

What are the characteristics of confidence? In essence it's about having an expectancy of success. You believe in yourself. Having confidence will lead to having an ability to concentrate well, to exert control, to set yourself personal goals from game to game and to measure them and to persist in your efforts to reach your potential.

Confidence is one of the most important characteristics of being a competent and respected umpire – one that players, coaches and colleagues will look forward to seeing and working with.

TIP Grasp every moment to make friends and influence people – before the game, during the game and after the game. The more effort you put in, the bigger your reward. Try to be confident and friendly and you will find that it becomes easier. Smile and someone will smile back at you!

Goal Setting

Goal-setting is identifying what you want to do and achieve. It is important that your goals are realistic and that they are measurable. Goals help you determine what is important, they increase your attention, focus your concentration and they have a major role to play in maintaining and increasing your level of motivation.

Some examples of valuable goals to set include, staying calm under pressure, being brave when you have to make that big decision in the dying minutes of the game (for some this is a nightmare!) or looking confident at all times.

It is important to make your goals positive. It sometimes helps to write them down. Make sure they are challenging but also realistic e.g there is little point in setting yourself a goal of one day umpiring an Olympic final; you need first to get yourself as highly qualified as you can in your own country.

Chapter 3

MATCH MANAGEMENT

Management remains at the forefront of the modern game in the list of 'desirable umpiring skills'. It has been the 'buzz word' in assessing performance since 2002 but it really 'kicked in' just before the Athens Olympic Games in 2004. Now, in 2012, everyone knows that there is a strong need for umpires to have good management skills if they are going to succeed.

So, what are management skills and how do we apply them to our umpiring? Managers are required to lead, to facilitate, to support, encourage and where necessary instruct, to work together, to compromise, to see that rules are applied across a workplace, to build a framework that generates confidence and worth and to take responsibility. They are also expected to be accountable.

Isn't that exactly what umpiring is all about? We do lead, facilitate, we do instruct, work together, compromise, apply rules, aim to generate fairness, confidence and worth, take responsibility and, perhaps most importantly, we are accountable. We have no one to blame or point the finger at when we make the wrong decision because between the two of us we make all the decisions…or do we? It's an interesting debate for a clubhouse after a game!

We need to plan and prepare if we are expected to manage effectively. A crucial part of our planning is the pre-match chat. In this very important time, we consider how to manage the game ahead of us. We close out any pre-conceived ideas we might have and we concentrate on the 'job' at hand. We think about the importance of being consistent, how we will communicate together and with the players, what we will do to help and support each other and how we will be a compliment to the game as opposed to running risk of spoiling it.

TIP When the play requires us to be sympathetic we should be. When a situation deserves a little humility we should demonstrate it. If we understand the players intentions and as long as fairness is maintained, a little shrug of the shoulders and opening of the hands is a very positive way of saying 'hey, I'm sorry, I know you tried to avoid the offence, but I've got to give this free hit' or, if the reaction to a big penalty you award suggests you've got it seriously wrong, hold your hand up, stop time, smile and confirm that you'll check with your colleague straight away. Always be approachable and never be aggressive. Be open, not closed…

Some easy to try examples of good management could include:

1   When setting-up a penalty corner, if you see an attacker or attackers with a foot or feet on the line or looking likely to break into the circle before the ball is played, point it out to them, smile and say 'stay outside the line' or 'don't break early'. Get the PC organised so as it can be the advantage it was intended to be.

2 Keeping a watchful eye on risk areas or incidents off the ball is always worthwhile. Glancing across the line of the probable pass will enable you to spot potential problems before they get more serious and it's much easier to keep the play moving, while using your voice to handle the off ball threat and put in a signal that clearly tells the players involved to ease off, calm down and take care.

3 The 5 metres rule is a really important one. If you get it right and apply it consistently it reduces whistle by creating space, it enhances flow, and importantly for you personally, it reduces pressure and risk of conflict. Let the 5m rule be one that you always manage well.

Those are just three examples but there are so many that you could consider adopting as a part of your personal goals list for the future.

Managing Conflict

Conflict can have a negative effect on performance and often its magnitude is hugely out of proportion to the disagreement that caused it. One of the interesting things about conflict on a hockey pitch (between players or coaches and the umpires) is that we have the same goals but sometimes disagree on the means by which they can be achieved.

What causes conflict between players or coaches and umpires?

The players will say inconsistency, lack of understanding, poor communication, the use of excessive authority. Inexperience is another cause – perhaps one that isn't as widely acknowledged as it should be?

The coaches will say all of the above and perhaps they will add lack of commitment, lack of effort or lack of fitness.

Unmanaged conflict can and often does damage relationships, so it is important that we all have the knowledge and the skills to manage it effectively. Communication skills are so important to the process.

How can the umpire manage conflict?

TIP Immediately a conflict begins try to resolve it. Don't ignore it and let it get worse. The worse it gets the more difficult it will become to manage and the more risk there is of it increasing your anxiety and therefore having a negative effect on your concentration and your performance.

TIP A touch of good humour or humility can often help to diffuse conflict or a difficult situation. Try it!

23

Chapter 4

COMMON SENSE -
THE UNWRITTEN RULE

Before we consider the real rules of the game, there is value in exploring one of the unwritten rules. Common sense is considered by many as the most important, (albeit invisible), rule in the hockey rules book.

All of us use common sense. There are so many occasions when the best decision we make, the most sensible, the most applauded, the most remembered is one that is purely based on common sense. It doesn't exist in print, there's no written reference but you know and everyone else knows that it was the 'CS Rule'…and most of the time the players and coaches welcome it and they appreciate it.

An example of common sense

⟩ The player chases 40 metres to play the ball and it just pops off the back-line before he reaches it. He lets off an expletive (wouldn't you after sprinting for nothing for 40m?). Don't measure the expletive as an offence, measure it as a reaction to his effort and frustration and show a bit of sympathy, not a green card. This is common sense and this is good management. A smile and a quiet 'hard luck but keep the swearing quiet if you can' will benefit everyone. Giving a warning card is not the best decision.

TIP Don't worry about using common sense. On occasions it's a 'needs must' situation and it's arguably better than the 'letter of the law'. Dealing with a difficult injury could be a good example. Once in a while it is the best thing to do. Most of us do it in every game without even realising it!

TIP If the conflict has resulted in you saying to a coach or a player 'hey let's talk it through in the bar or the club after the game' (and this often does temporarily resolve the situation), be calm, try to feel and look confident, be receptive, listen first, don't be defensive and always acknowledge the other persons point of view.

The key is to do all you can to find some common ground, to be respectful of differences and opinions, but don't compromise the rules or the spirit of the game.

If you have good management skills, everyone will benefit; the players and the coaches, the spectators…the game and last but not least…you.

Chapter 5

FITNESS - MOBILITY & POSITIONING

Fit, mobile and well positioned umpires are better able to concentrate on the flow of the match and on the decisions that need to be made.

Umpiring is far more enjoyable when you are fit. Good fitness and an ability to 'read' the game will enable you to be in the right position and to keep up with the speed of todays hockey.

Umpires are known to cover up to 5km during a 70 minutes match. The total distance covered can vary and is dependent on the nature of the match – some are end to end and others sometimes get caught up in the midfield. The intensity of the work can also vary considerably, regardless of the total distance covered.

The total work performed comprises of a variety of 'modes of work' that determine the physical demands. These modes include various types of motion; walking, jogging, cruising and sprinting, which are performed forwards, backwards and sideways. This is known as functional running and is punctuated with stopping, starting, accelerating and decelerating.

In addition, a certain amount of time is spent standing and there are stationary positions commonly assumed by umpires. These enhance viewing and can sometimes include the sideways lunge and the squat position to varying depths...albeit the more experienced coaches will tell the more experienced umpires that they don't need to squat! They are encouraged to stay upright and move their feet to enable them to see.

So...do you take your umpiring fitness seriously? It is an important part of your performance and the higher you aim or climb on the umpiring ladder, the more prominence you give it. Endurance should be developed in the pre-season and maintained during the season, while speed and agility are the core components to your success.

There are a number of ways of developing your fitness for umpiring. Some umpires train with the players at the club, some prefer to do it alone at the gym or running or swimming. The most important thing is to do something; be serious about it. Take your fitness from 'OK' to 'good' and know that the fitter you are, the better your concentration will be, your mobility and your performance will measurably improve and all of this leads to higher reward.

Improving your Mobility

Umpires must be mobile so as they can move to appropriate positions throughout the match.

There are a number of ways to improve your mobility. One of the biggest difficulties when you start umpiring is actually recognising what good mobility is. Is it running around needlessly? Is it about being able to cover short distances quickly and effortlessly? Is it about good balance, appearing poised and not heavy or awkward?

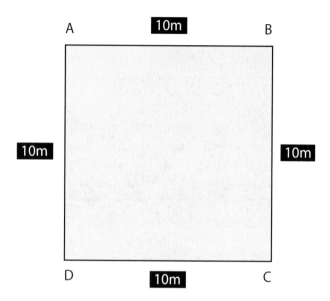

The key is to practice and a good start is to set up a square with each side measuring 10 metres in length. You should have sides or points A, B, C and D. Your aim is to replicate what you do on the pitch. Face the centre of the square at all times, assume the ball and play is in the centre and run sideways from point (corner) A to point B. At point B, turn and run backwards to point C (keep your focus on the centre of the square) and when you arrive at point C, turn and run sideways again to point D.

At point D, turn and sprint to point A. Your agility and speed will improve as you practice and you are recommended to do 3 circuits at maximum speed, take a 1 minute beak and then repeat. You will often see the international umpires using this practice immediately prior to tournaments but it can be done alone in the park or at your local club pitch at any time.

It's a good warm-up exercise and can easily be set up using the lines as your guides. Don't forget to stretch fully before you start.

Good Positioning

Good positioning as a hockey umpire is about being in the right place at the right time. It's as easy as that. So where is the right place? Now it starts to become more difficult! There are two important rules to remember - stay out of the way of the players at all times and face the play at all times.

Each umpire operates mainly in half of the field with the centre line to their left. However, don't read this to mean that there is no need to go over the centre line into the other half

29

of the pitch because nothing is further from the truth. Every decision you make or should make requires credibility and you are responsible for your entire side-line so refraining from crossing the centre line when play is down in the far 23m area, is not acceptable. In addition, how can you assist your colleague (the other umpire) with play on the far side of their circle or coming out of their circle if you are on the other side of the centre line?

Coaches will talk to you about two different types of positioning; **open play** and at **set-pieces**. In open play, the most suitable position for umpires is recognised as ahead of the play and on the right of the attacking team. This doesn't mean ahead of the highest positioned attacking player... rather the play. You are recommended to be within 5 metres of your side-line, moving further in when necessary (when play is on the far side of the field) and moving out when necessary (when play is coming or going down your side of the pitch). Moving out will increase your arc of vision. Having a good angle is important and it helps you to avoid having to make a decision 'from the back of the train'. You can't ever see the driver if you look through all the carriages can you?

When play is in your 23 metres area and approaching your circle, you must move further into the field away from the side lines and closer or into the circle itself. This is good positioning and it will allow you to see important offences and to judge whether shots at goal are legitimate or if the ball has wholly crossed the goal line.

Set piece positioning is where you position yourself while a penalty commences. Examples are corners, penalty corners, penalty strokes, or free hits to either team.

For a penalty stroke, you should be approximately 2 metres behind and slightly to the right of the taker.

For a penalty corner you need to be very conscious of the potential of the play. In other words, be aware of the players who may be running in and the player who may be running directly at you! There are more players in or close to the circle at a penalty corner than at any other time and they are likely to be buzzing in all directions. It is essential that you don't get in the way but you need to be in there and able to see as much as possible. Moving once the ball is played is the best advice you can be given. Don't get caught standing still and do your best to avoid being square with the play – it makes it so much harder to see what's happening.

For penalty corners taken on the far side of your circle, consider being in line with or just outside your near post and approximately 2 metres into the pitch. For penalty corners on your near side (not very common) think about being level with the edge of the circle and again about 2 metres into the pitch from the back line. When the ball is injected, move towards the best spot without impeding the players and remember you will need to see as much as possible so try to open up your shoulders and take in the widest arc of vision.

> **TIP** Think about trying to keep the corner flag in line with the middle of your back. This will help you avoid being flat and burdened with an unnecessarily narrow view. It will open up your arc of vision and reduce the number of occasions you have your back to the back line or the side line; something that will mean you are constantly turning your head to see and therefore potentially taking your eyes off the play.

For **corners** (commonly known as long corners), on your near side, step off the back line and aim to be approximately in line with the edge of the circle and moving towards the PC marker as the ball travels across. For corners on the far side, 2 metres off the near post into the pitch is a good starting point but it will always depend on the players and their movement between you and the ball. Some umpires like to be closer to the top of the circle edge so as to see across more clearly. The key is to let the play determine your position and be aware of the support that your colleague can and should give you (see next paragraph).

What about penalty corners at the other end of the pitch and penalty strokes too? You will be a very visible assistant for the penalty stroke (on the back line and between 7 and 10 metres from the post) but for a penalty corner, you are less visible while still having an important role to play. The best place to stand is over the centre line by 5 metres or so and in or close to the centre of the pitch. Make sure you discuss your supporting position with your colleague before the game commences. Bear in mind that among the requirements or expectations for you as the supporting umpire is that you can see if the shot at goal is inside or outside of the post when it strikes the unlucky defenders foot!

Chapter 6

THE LANGUAGE OF THE GAME

The purpose of this chapter is to identify the terms as used by the coaches and players. The aim is to increase understanding, particularly for the less experienced umpire; perhaps someone who hasn't played hockey prior to taking up the whistle.

Hit: This is the action of swinging the stick to propel the ball - usually with the hands positioned together.

Push: A pass made with the stick on the ground and in contact with the ball until the pass is made - usually with the hands apart.

Slap: This action also involves the stick being on the ground but while it starts with the stick behind the ball, this time it is not in contact with it. The motion is the stick slapping through the ball on an arc in contact with the ground, making this a quicker more powerful and faster action than the push.

Flick: This term describes the action of lifting the ball powerfully. Used for shorter distances e.g. shot at goal.

Aerial Ball (Scoop): Lifting the ball a longer distance with the stick – can be 20 to 60 metres (hoisting or throwing are terms commonly used to describe this action).

Moving the Ball (the pass): Sending the ball with the stick towards a player on their team.

Movement off the Ball: This is a very common call from the coach and it represents the action of running to create space and options for players to receive passes, make passes and confuse opponents.

Moving with the Ball: This describes the player moving with the ball on or very close to the stick, (sometimes called a dribble).

Open stick - (forehand): Moving with the ball, stick at an angle (approx 45 °) on the ground and in contact with the ball - carrying it to where the player can have the vision to see most passes.

Reverse stick - (backhand): The same action as described above but with the stick on the reverse side.

Jab Tackle: The jab can be used as a form of delay either to dispossess a player with the ball if the ball is away from the stick or to tempt the player to take their eyes off the ball and possibly lose possession.

The stick held in the left hand jabs out towards the ball and then returns to both hands. This is often used to make the player with the ball put their eyes down and lose concentration. It is not necessarily used to get the ball.

Open side block tackle - forehand tackle: Using a strong low, body position the player attempts to take the ball from the opponent.

Reverse stick tackle - backhand tackle: This describes the action of trying to take the ball from an opponent on the reverse side.

Shave Tackle: 'Stealing' the ball from the side with a quick 'shaving action' stick on the ground flat and using the

35

hook - without touching the stick of the opponent.

Channelling: Channelling is the action of a defending player preventing an attacker entering space, usually a direct line to goal. It refers to one of two things; either keeping the player out to the side of the pitch or forcing the player towards another defending player so as they can make the tackle.

Marking: Marking means tracking individual players and covering space through which passes can be made. It is an important aspect of the game with defenders attempting to stop an attacker gaining possession of the ball.

Marking will generally be from the side or slightly in front for most of the pitch, with the defender trying to intercept the ball.

Covering: A free player behind the 'action' , ready to step in if required to take the ball.

Double Teaming: The tactical action made by a coach to stop a very influential player on the opposition. It involves placing two players to 'take care' of this opponent. One player marks 'person to person' and the other is used to intercept a pass to that player.

Attacking: When a team is in attack there should be width, depth, support and overload– all members of the team contribute to the attack, maintaining shape and position and running into spaces to receive passes.

Defending: When a team has lost possession the players will work to regain the ball and deny space to the attackers. This may be with the forwards chasing back to put pressure on the opposition or the defenders 'stepping up' to close down the forwards and cut off options to run with the ball or pass. The more experienced defenders delay and show patience to regain possession – ensuring they do not rush towards the ball (squeeze the opposition is a term sometimes used).

Press: The word 'press' is used to describe putting pressure on the team in possession of the ball.

Rebound: The act of following up a shot at goal can be a flick / slap / hit / push at goal.

Penalty Corner Injection: A term used to describe the ball being put into play at a penalty corner.

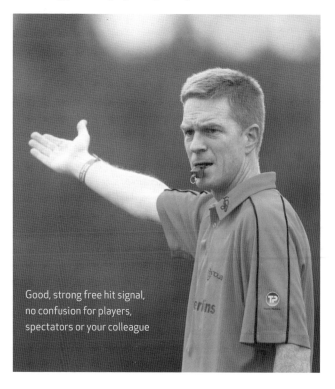

Good, strong free hit signal, no confusion for players, spectators or your colleague

Chapter 7

MATCH PREPARATION

In this chapter we consider how to prepare immediately before a game commences. We all prepare differently. Some umpires like to have time alone to listen to music or read a book and they stay in their car or go and find a quiet corner somewhere prior to meeting their colleague; others like to socialise with people and prefer to go into the clubhouse or coffee lounge area where casual conversation can be had. There are also those who want to talk only about the basics (not always best) and others who like to detail and consider every single possible scenario (not ideal either). The key is to recognise and respect the importance of good preparation and be prepared to manage the discussion. You are a team and you both have a duty to be as good as you can in every game and that requires some planning. If your colleague isn't as forthcoming as you would like or suggests things that make you nervous rather than confident, deal with them. Don't let it turn into a crisis!

Umpires should make every effort to be at the venue an hour before the match is due to start, however sometimes this simply isn't possible – perhaps you were a player in the match that was immediately before. Whatever your circumstances, recognise that while your own personal preparation is very important, you really must do all you can to prepare together and your preparation as a pair of umpires will require you to talk some things through and plan how you will be fair, consistent and a team. If you don't do this and talk only about which side of the field you will take and who will time each half, you will risk letting the players and yourselves down.

Your 'meeting' before the match is commonly known as the **pre-match chat** and if it is possible, you should plan in a minimum of 15 minutes of your time. We explore the content in more detail later in the chapter.

When the chat is complete there are other duties to be undertaken. If time is tight, why not combine the two? You need to check the pitch markings, the goals, the run-off areas, the corner flags and make sure that the nets are in good order. You also need to confirm if there are team benches for the substitutes to sit on and sin-bins for any offenders who are temporarily suspended during the game (two chairs will normally suffice – just away from the two benches and at the centre line about 4 or 5 metres back from the edge of the pitch).

Then it's time to whistle up the captains to toss a coin and decide which team will take the ball (the centre pass) and which will choose ends (which end of the pitch to attack or defend). The winner of the toss has the first choice.

> **TIP** Use an interesting coin for the toss. It always makes a nice ice-breaker and brings a smile to the faces of the players.

TIP Try to get the toss underway promptly. If it's possible, aim for 15 minutes before the start time. Too often, umpires call the captains to toss the coin with only seconds remaining…the captain is busy briefing the team, or the team are going through the last 'crucial' penalty corner drills… bad timing umpire…not the best start to your game!

The Pre-Match Talk (chat)

Here are some clues as to what to discuss. You may want to add to them. This is not a definitive list.

> You are the "third team" on the pitch – how will you work together? Penalty corners are a great starting point.

> How will you be consistent and fair?

> How will you communicate and help each other and the players?

> What happens if it all goes horribly wrong? (You can't run away!)

> What about advantage and flow? (You should not blow the whistle unnecessarily.)

> What about the lifted ball (you blow it only if it's dangerous) and the aerial ball – always contentious unfortunately. It's wise to get it right and essential to be consistent.

> What about applying the 5m Rule? (You must try to get that space for the players and be consistent with your interpretation all over the pitch.)

> Are you both confident of your application of the intricacies of the self-pass rule? Do you recognise and

penalise channelling if it interferes with the play (i.e. when the opposing player was less than 5m away as the pass was taken)?

〉 Who will bring time back in, (signal readiness for the re-start), when it has been stopped because of injury or incident?

〉 How about eye-contact... particularly in and around the circles? (This is very important to you working together effectively. It is essential to your game plan – your management and your control.)

〉 What about warning cards?

〉 Will you help each other with play coming out of the circles on your side of the pitch?

〉 Do either of you have any confusing or self-made signals?

In addition, there are less important things to discuss. These include who will take which side of the pitch and who will time the first half.

As you can see, the value of arriving at the venue within plenty of time is genuine. If you seriously want to perform well and be of benefit to the match, you must get there early and spend quality time discussing and planning with your colleague.

Chapter 8

THE RULES OF THE GAME

The International Hockey Federation (FIH) regularly reviews the Rules of Hockey The rules are made by the FIH Hockey Rules Commitee; a group of people with experience from all areas of hockey. Some have been international players, others international umpires, coaches, administrators or officials. Together they consult with the affiliated national associations to produce a blend of expertise.

There is no doubt that hockey is seen as an innovative and creative sport. Rules that no longer contribute positively to the game are removed. New rules are introduced regularly and always they lead to increased speed and the development of new skills. We have no offside so we have no opportunity for the defence to dictate to the attack. We have the self-pass. What a wonderful difference that has made to our sport and at the highest levels of international hockey, we have video technology that allows not only the umpires but also the teams to make referrals to the video umpire. Fantastic!

In 2013, hockey has 14 Rules and one of those (the first) is exclusively to do with the field of play, how long the pitch is, how wide it is and what the pitch markings are for.

For us as umpires this information is not the most important. We know the pitch is twice as long as it is wide, we know that the shooting circles are big and we need them to be visible (for the lines to be clear and not scuffed out), we know there is a centre line, two back lines and two 23m lines. We hope, particularly now in 2013, that the pitch will have the broken 5m line surrounding each circle so as to assist the players and ourselves with the self pass rule and measuring the 5m requirement. Internationally these broken lines are mandatory. In England they are mandatory for all national league matches and on any new or re-furbished pitch.

Everything else in this rule is, in the bigger scheme of things, trivial and of little interest to umpires.

The Composition of Teams

Until 2007 there was a mandatory requirement to have a goalkeeper on the field of play at all times. The game could not be played unless both teams had a goalkeeper on the pitch. The Hockey Rules Commitee made a brave decision and changed it. It brought the teams more flexibility and it brought more excitement to the sport.

The options that this change has brought to the game are:

1 Each team may play with a goalkeeper with goalkeeping privileges wearing full protective equipment comprised of at least headgear, leg guards and kickers and a different coloured shirt; or

2 Each team may play with a goalkeeper with goalkeeping privileges wearing only protective headgear and a different coloured shirt (commonly known as a 'kicking back'); or

3 Each team may play with only field players and no player with goalkeeping privileges and therefore no player wearing protective headgear or different coloured shirt.

TIP Time is stopped for substitution of goalkeepers wearing fully protective equipment but not for other substitutions. Umpires should not stop time if the goalkeeper is coming off to be replaced with a field player and this shouldn't be a problem because the goalkeeper can leave the pitch over the back-line.

Captains

For umpires perhaps the most important element of this rule is that captains are responsible for the behaviour of all players on their team. This includes the substitutes. If the team is from a small club, it is entirely possible that they will have only one or two substitutes and in some cases they may have none at all. In a match involving bigger clubs there may be five (the maximum number is five).

There are occasions when the substitute players like to umpire the game or at least call the offences for us! Sometimes when they think we have missed something or made the wrong call (decision) they have an overwhelming need to tell us (and often everyone else) in a very loud voice! This is not helpful, however, unless it becomes a real hindrance most umpires 'turn a deaf ear' or occasionally stop the game at a convenient time and ask the captain 'to have a word'!

TIP When and if the substitute players or any player on the field, slip below the level of good conduct, the umpire should not hesitate to try and regain order and discipline and the most effective way to do this is to stop the time and call the captain of the offending team over. Go towards the captain and aim to meet them half way in distance terms. Act firmly but calmly. Advise them that in the interest of the game, you require them to speak with their player/s and ask them to tone down their criticism at very least. Tell them you don't want to warn or suspend players for this type of misconduct but you will if things do not change. You will normally need to allow the captain to gather the players in and give them the message and then resume the game with composure and control.

TIP Once you have 'used' the captain to help you restore good conduct you should consider it done…no second chances. If you have told them that you will take more serious action if it continues, when and if it does, you must. Idle threats lead to a loss of control. Don't let that happen.

Players Clothing and Equipment

The clothing element within this rule is very straightforward and is of little relevance to umpires. However, the equipment element is something that regularly causes a question or hesitation when offering an answer.

Here are some facts to help you:

⟩ Field players are permitted to wear gloves as long as they don't significantly increase the natural size of the hands.

> Field players are recommended to wear shin, ankle and mouth protection. Note the word is recommended. None of these items are mandatory. (Note that in some junior competitions in England there are mandatory requirements – always check the competition regulations.)

> When defending penalty corners, defenders are permitted to wear a smooth, preferably transparent or white but otherwise dark, plain coloured face mask that fits flush with the face. The mask must be removed immediately following the penalty corner or, to clarify, when the penalty corner rules cease to apply i.e. when the ball has passed beyond 5m of the circle edge. These masks may also be worn when defending a penalty stroke.

> Field players are permitted to wear a smooth, preferably transparent or white but otherwise dark plain coloured face mask which fits flush with the face, soft protective head covering or eye protection in the form of plastic goggles for the duration of the match if, and only if, they have a medical reason for doing so. An example of this could be a fractured cheek bone.

> Only fully protected goalkeepers are permitted to wear body, upper arm, elbow, forearm, hand and thigh protectors, leg guards and kickers. For a field player adopting the role of a goalkeeper, the permitted equipment is protective headgear incorporating a helmet with fixed full face protection and cover for the entire head.

> **TIP** Goalkeepers must wear a shirt that is a different colour to the team players. On occasions you will get onto the pitch to discover that the goalkeeper's shirt is the same colour as your own. Nine times out of ten the teams won't object and you can carry on regardless however, out of courtesy it is always worth asking the captains if they have an objection. If they do, and you as a team of umpires have alternative coloured shirts in your bag, the recommendation is that you change.

> Lastly, we will consider the hockey stick. There is a revised specification that will apply to all international hockey from January 2013, however it won't be introduced to hockey in England until September 2013 . (Full details can be found in the Hockey Rules book – see pages 55-60.) A new device is to be made available to Technical Officials to measure the bow of the stick. Umpires shouldn't consider this to be their responsibility.

Starting and Re-starting the Match

Once you are happy that both teams are ready to play and you have checked the goals, the nets, the corner flags and all of the other pitch equipment, the game can commence. It is important that you don't get caught unawares and that you are fully focused. Be absolutely sure that you know which colour team is going in which direction – silly as this seems there are occasions when umpires forget and then make an unnecessary and embarrassing error.

The person taking the centre pass is permitted to play the ball in any direction and they can self-pass. Be prepared umpires, this rule has made a very significant impact on the game in all areas of play. You need to be sharper and more aware of the potential of play at all times. Look around and see what might happen.

At the centre pass, until the ball is played, all other players must remain in their own half of the field. Players from the same team as the pass taker must be a minimum of 1m from the ball and players from the opposing team must be a minimum of 5m from the ball.

> **TIP** Don't be too distant at the start of the game. Position yourself about 5-7m into the pitch and have your 23m line to your right. Prepare yourself for the self pass to be played right from the start of the game.

On occasions the game is re-started with a bully. The bully appears to have been a part of hockey forever, and when you talk about the game to people who don't follow hockey closely it is always the bully that they remember!

As the Rules currently stand, the game can be re-started with a bully for any one of three reasons:

1 Following a simultaneous offence by players of opposing teams.

2 Following an accident or incident from which there was no offence.

3 If the ball has to be replaced.

It is important to remember that the bully cannot be taken within 14.63m of the back-line, (the radius of the shooting circle).

TIP The players are often unfamiliar with this Rule. If there is an incident requiring a bully and it's within 14.63m of the back-line (top of the circle), step in promptly, remove the confusion and advise them where it is to be taken.

TIP Although the fundamental characteristics of the 'bully' have been retained for many years, things have moved on! The rule has been simplified and now the sticks are required to touch only once.

Ball outside the Field of Play

The lines are a part of play. The circle lines are a part of the shooting circles. For the ball to be measured as being out of play, it has to **completely** cross the side-lines or back-lines. This is often difficult to see and most players tend to think that they can see it more clearly than you can. It emphasises the importance of not being too distant from play. Balls going off the side-line or back-line should not be contentious… they should be obvious.

> **TIP** One of the most common causes of umpire errors on the sides of the pitch (down the channels) is due to a failure to move out (off of the pitch), and create a suitable angle to see the play...all of the play. Too often umpires stay directly behind the line of play and they make it very difficult for themselves. Move out umpires...aim for 45 degree angles of vision when the play is wide and particularly when it is going away from you.

When the ball is played over the **back-line** and no goal is scored:

> If it was played by an attacker, the umpire should award a hit-out. It should be taken in line with where it crossed the back-line and into the pitch up to 15m from the back-line.

> If it was played unintentionally by a defender or deflected by a goal-keeper, the umpire should award a corner.

> If it was played unintentionally by a defender or deflected by a goalkeeper, the umpire should award a corner.

Method of Scoring

The best goals and the most exciting goals are those that take everyone by surprise. However, umpires are not supposed to be surprised! The most difficult thing is to see who, in a very crowded circle, last struck the ball before it entered the goal. Was it an attacking player or was it a defending player? Sometimes there can be a melee of players and it is practically impossible to see who last touched it. Until September 2012 for a goal to be scored the ball had to be played or last touched by an attacker inside the circle. Now we have a new mandatory experimental rule in place and for umpires it is a treat! The rule is: a goal is scored when the ball is played by

an attacker, or touches the stick or body of a defender, within the circle. The 'own goal' has arrived at last!

Conduct of Play - Players

This is Rule 9 and it's lengthy! It's full of 'must nots' and just as you think you know them all, it develops into Rule 10 which is another list of 'must not's, but this time they are specific to goalkeepers or players with goalkeeping privileges.

As umpires when we are asked about conduct, we might reply that we expect the players to act responsibly at all times. However, in the real world, nothing is quite that easy. This is probably the exact reason that this rule has so many parts to it (17 in all).

Helpfully in almost all cases within the Rules, there is a guidance reference or an example recorded in italics alongside most of these 'must nots'.

We will examine some of the areas within the rule, but not all. To begin we will consider Rule 9.6 and this reads that players must not **hit** the ball **hard** on the forehand with the edge of the stick. This has caused some confusion and a number of umpires ask "what is hard, is there a definitive answer available?" The interesting thing is that players are permitted to hit the ball hard on the reverse side (the back hand) with the edge of the stick, so it begs the question, why not the forehand? The answer is that the reverse side is measured as having developed as a technical skill. It is permitted subject to danger. The use of the forehand is more open to error as there is more risk of it being poorly controlled. To strike it in a controlled way, the player needs to be very precise in the strike. The ball and stick contact area needs to be almost exact to guarantee that it actually goes where intended. So, to remove the risk, the rule has been introduced. The forehand edge hit is regularly used as a controlled action in a tackle to raise the ball over an opponents stick or over a goalkeeper who is lying on the ground.

Another 'must not' that can sometimes be confusing particularly for the players is that they must not lift their stick over the heads of other players. They often do this because they are unexpectedly obstructed. The very first time this happens in a game, blow the whistle, use your voice and make a signal to tell the player to keep their stick down then award them the free hit because they were obstructed. This is the correct decision for the umpire to make in this circumstance because the obstruction was the *first* offence. However, if the players persist with the stick over the head business, it will mean a change of tactic and after repeated cautions you should use a warning card.

Rule 9.10 reads that players must not approach within 5 metres of an opponent receiving a falling raised ball until it has been received, controlled and is on the ground. This is a rule that has troubled players, coaches and umpires alike. Inconsistency is all too evident!

The falling raised ball is commonly known as the aerial ball. The term refers to a ball that is intentionally raised and travels high over a long distance. It is a very skilful piece of play and has become increasingly evident in all areas of the game; defenders use it to get out of trouble and midfielders use it to set up the attack – to bypass the opposition by sailing the ball over the top of them.

Unfortunately the reality is that the ball doesn't always fall into the intended space and on occasions, there are two or more players underneath it. It is here that we umpires often struggle to see who was there first and therefore who was best positioned to receive the ball. It becomes a distraction for the umpire and the result is that there is often inconsistency and yet, the rule is simple. It reads "If it is not clear which player is the initial receiver, the player of the team that raised the ball must allow the opponent to receive it."

> **TIP** Don't wait for the ball to fall between the players. Assess the position quickly and if it's apparent that neither player is going to back off and give the other the time and space, blow the whistle and award the free hit. This will mean you prevent the danger by whistling immediately the ball starts to descend – much better than reacting too late…

Conduct of Play - Goalkeepers and players with goalkeeping privileges

This is relatively straight forward, albeit it has changed substantially in recent years. The main element of change is that there doesn't have to be a goalkeeper on the pitch (as referenced earlier in this chapter - see Composition of Teams).

The important things for us umpires to note are that a kitted goalkeeper (one who wears protective equipment comprising of at least headgear, leg guards and kickers) is restricted to participating in the game in their own 23m area only; unless they are taking a penalty stroke. For a goalkeeper wearing only protective headgear and a shirt of another colour, when wearing the headgear they can play (participate) in their own defending 23m area only, but if they remove that headgear (which they can) they can participate anywhere on the field.

TIP Players with goalkeeping privileges must wear protective headgear when defending a penalty stroke or a penalty corner.

The change that continues to grab headlines is the one that permits the goalkeeper (when the ball is in their circle) to use their stick, **hands, arms or any part of their body** to push the ball away, to deflect it in any direction including over the back-line, or to stop it. This is considerably different to the old rule. However the necessary clarification is recorded immediately below the rule. It reads "This permits a goalkeeper to use their hands, arms or any other part of their body to move the ball away **but only as part of a goal saving action and not to propel the ball forcefully so that it travels a long distance**". So, don't panic umpires and don't get excited goalkeepers! There is no room for a goalie to flick the ball up off the kicker and then bat it 50m up the pitch with the hand at 150km an hour!

It does mean that they can, when lying on the ground in front of the goal, use the hand to push or sweep away the ball that's been shot at the goal. It also means that they can, when moving towards or into a shot, propel it forwards with the hand. Note that this is not 'forcefully over a long distance' and therefore is completely within the rule.

Conduct of Play - Umpires

This rule outlines the responsibilities of the umpires. It refers to them being the judges of fair play. It confirms when they should blow the whistle. It reminds them that they are responsible for decisions in their own circle, tells them that

55

they must not coach the players while umpiring, confirms when they should stop or re-start the game and so on. Interestingly, there is no reference to the two umpires being expected to work together as a team. Perhaps this is because there is an assumption that they will be the third team on the pitch and will work together to ensure that the game is played in the right spirit and with consistency. They will be consistent and the decisions will be balanced and the same at both ends of the pitch and if one umpire does miss an offence, the other will pick it up.

TIP One of the strongest tools an umpire has is eye-contact; firstly to demonstrate confidence in their decisions and secondly to look at each other and offer supporting or assisting signals when they are required.   You can never have too much of it!

TIP When you are the disengaged umpire you should refrain from signaling offences in the engaged umpires area of the pitch until they look to you for assistance. To signal for a penalty corner in your colleagues circle before they have sought assistance, is not the way forward! Always talk about your eye contact and assistance in your pre-match chat. You should be able to rely on each other for help for the benefit of the game – not feel threatened or intimidated by each other.

Chapter 9

PENALTIES AND PROCEDURES

The opening line in this rule is a reference to an area that is deservedly getting more and more attention. The rule is 12.1 and it is **'advantage'**. The game is determined to move to a 'minimum interference' zone and the umpires are key to this. Today's hockey is growing ever faster and it neither wants nor deserves umpiring that unnecessarily interrupts the flow. All of us need to recognise the importance of knowing when **not** to blow the whistle as well as when to blow. It takes time and practise but it's worth the effort.

While taking all of this on board, it should be noted that now the self-pass is so evident and so well used, blowing an offence is often more of an advantage than 'holding' the whistle so don't let the players struggle unnecessarily… give them a quick whistle and a quick free if it looks like creating more of an advantage for them. It's like everything in officiating…getting the right balance is key.

Free-Hit

The revised free hit rule introduced in 2010 brought about the biggest change to hockey since the removal of offside. We had a mandatory experiment in place for two years to measure the feasibility of introducing the self pass and the experiment proved overwhelmingly successful. The self pass is here to stay and as a result the speed of play has increased dramatically…no more 'time for a breather' when a free hit is awarded…far from it! Umpires need to be **more** ahead of the play now, faster and fitter and able to quickly assess and recognise the options available to the players .

Listed below are the key principles.

> For free hits (including centre passes, corners and all sideline restarts after the ball has been outside the field), the ball must be stationary and all opponents must be at least 5 metres from it (the ball).

TIP If an opponent is within 5 metres of the ball (and with a quickly taken self pass they inevitably are), they must not interfere with the taking of the free hit nor play or attempt to play the ball and umpires, you should note that if the opponent is not playing the ball, attempting to play the ball or influencing play, the free hit need not be delayed or interrupted. Let them play!

TIP If an opponent makes no visible effort to retreat to the required distance or they knock the ball away or intentionally run over it or into the path of the taker, blow the whistle again and progress the free hit further up the pitch, (up to 10m), that is unless it is within the 23m area, in which case, if it is the defending side offending, you are within the Rules to upgrade the penalty and award a penalty corner. This type of action is intentional. It's purpose is to slow things down and we commonly refer to it as 'breaking down the play'. It should be penalised strongly every time it happens. If you see it, blow your whistle loudly and give a clear message that's it's a once only offence…next time it will be penalised with a card .

> The player taking the free hit can use a hit, push, flick or scoop. The ball may be raised immediately using a push, flick or scoop but must not be raised intentionally using a hit.

> For free hits awarded to the attack within the 23 metres area, the ball must not be played into the circle until it has travelled at least 5 metres or has been touched by a player of either team other than the player taking the free hit.

If the player taking the free hit continues to play the ball (ie no other player has yet played it):

– that player may play the ball any number of times, but

– the ball must travel at least 5 metres, before

– that player plays the ball into the circle by hitting or pushing the ball again.

Alternatively:

– another player of either team who can legitimately play the ball must deflect, hit or push the ball before it enters the circle,

– or

– after this player has touched the ball, it can be played into the circle by any other player including the player who took the free hit.

TIP The introduction of the scoop or flick at a free hit may mean more use of the high ball across (above) the attacking circle so that it lands outside the circle. This is fine as long as it isn't dangerous.

TIP It makes no difference what 'level' of game it is, most of the time the players want to take the free-hit quickly, particularly now we have the self-pass option. Umpires, you will have heard it said many times, this is not the time to take a rest! Be prepared, get yourself into the best position to see whatever may come next and get there quickly. It is really important that you try to read the game at all times – particularly in crucial areas of the pitch. Stay ahead of the play. Best advice you can be given is to make sure you're always at least 5-7 metres ahead of it.

Corner

The umpire should award a corner when the ball is unintentionally played over the back-line by a defending player. It makes no difference where the defending player is positioned. They can be anywhere on the pitch. The key consideration is the word 'unintentional'.

The corner markers are 5m from the corners of the pitch, on the side-lines. Before the corner is taken, you should ensure that all players except the taker are at least 5m from the ball, and remember it's likely to be a self pass if 'nothing else is on'.

The corner must be taken from the side the ball crossed the back-line (i.e. near-side of the goal or far-side). If the ball crosses the back-line in the middle of the back-line i.e. over the cross-bar of the goal, it may be taken from either side. The attacking team make the decision.

Penalty Corner

The Penalty Corner Rule is perhaps the most complex of the Hockey Rules. There are many things to remember and potentially even more to see. One important thing to remember is that unlike the Corner Rule, a choice is available. The penalty corner can be taken from either side of the goal and the choice belongs with the attacking team.

Before the penalty corner is taken, the umpires need to ensure that everyone is correctly positioned. The goalkeeper and four defenders defend the goal and they can position themselves anywhere behind the back-line, on condition that they are a minimum of 5m from the ball. (There is a 5m marker on each side of the goal on the back-line.) The remaining players in the defending team should be on, or beyond, the centre-line. The attacking players can position themselves anywhere on the pitch outside of the attacking circle. As with the defence, they also must be a minimum of 5m from the ball prior to it being played.

> **TIP** Manage the set-up effectively. Be in charge and be helpful! Recognise that it is increasingly common for defending players to wear protective face-masks at PCs. Give them time to kit themselves up but don't allow them to 'fiddle about' for ever! Internationally the aim is for PCs to be taken within 40 seconds of being awarded.

Once the defenders are in position there should be an expectation for the PC to commence. 'Huddles' by the attack on the top of the circle are increasingly evident and if the defenders are ready, the attackers huddle can hold up the play unnecessarily. Intervene umpires and advise the attack that you won't allow them to hold it up again. Manage delays of this nature out of the game from the start.

So what are the main things to look for as the controlling umpire at a penalty corner?

Let's keep this simple.

1 Look for your colleague and ensure that they are in-tune with you and ready to help if required...to be the extra pair of eyes.

2 Look at the defence and ensure that they have the correct number of players taking up their positions behind the back-line and if they are putting on protective facemasks, they do it as quickly as is reasonable.

3 Look at the attack and this should include the taker (the person injecting the penalty corner into the circle). Make sure all are in position and that the taker has at least one foot outside of the field of play.

4 Before you allow the PC to commence, look to see that you are out of everyone's way and then give the taker the 'ok' to play. You can do this with a nod or by lowering your arm.

5 Look to see that no defender crosses the back-line before the ball is played and that everyone (attack and defence) are a minimum of 5m from the taker.

What is the role of the assisting umpire at a penalty corner?

This in the opinion of many coaches is when the umpiring team should function to capacity i.e. genuinely and proactively work together to ensure that no offence is missed. What we have to recognise is that the number of players in and around the circle is usually high (a minimum of 12) and it's all too easy to miss something so the extra pair of eyes is essential.

The assisting umpire should be prepared, supportive and focused. He or she should be in a 'positive' position, over the centre line and at an angle that allows clear vision of the defenders running out, the goal, and being realistic, as much of the play as possible. If the controlling umpire misses something that needs to be penalised the process should be fluid and calm. The assisting signal should be big, high and clear and should only be offered when eye contact is made. If the pre-match chat is as good as it needs to be, the planning is done and the delivery is easy.

TIP FOR THE CONTROLLING UMPIRE:

While the PC is being set up, as it approaches the almost ready stage, it's useful to position yourself towards the middle of the goal a couple of metres into the pitch and hold one arm up high from the shoulder. Try not to look like an officious traffic policeman....casual but in control is wise! The purpose of your signal is to advise the taker to wait until everyone is ready at which stage you will drop your arm. Speak to the taker and make sure they understand and will look to you before injecting the ball and very importantly, don't drop your arm until you've taken up your position. This means of communicating readiness is useful to everyone, defence and attack alike. As soon as everyone is ready, step back into your position and then lower your arm. Be warned... don't lower your arm until you are in position – lowering it indicates that the penalty corner can commence. And one further little tip; occasionally you don't have a lot of time. You should avoid being seen to hold up the play. Under no circumstances should the players have to wait for you!

When should a penalty corner be awarded?

Pending advantage, there are 5 circumstances. They are:

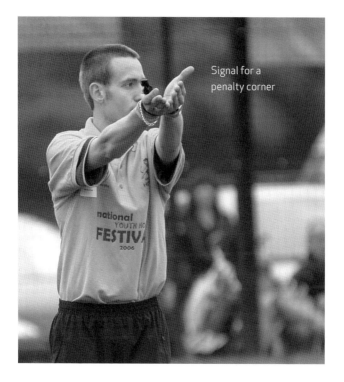

Signal for a
penalty corner

1 A defending player intentionally playing the ball over the defending back-line from anywhere on the pitch.

2 An intentional offence by a defending player outside of their circle but inside of their defending 23m area.

3 An offence by a defending player in the circle, which does not prevent the probable scoring of a goal.

TIP Consider the word 'intentional'. Hard or clumsy tackles are not intentional offences and should not be penalised as intentional offences. In these circumstances, a free-hit is the correct penalty.

65

TIP Tell yourself "I must see the ball at all times" and this will encourage and help you to position yourself well. Sometimes it can be difficult in a busy and heavily populated circle especially at a corner or penalty corner…there's a lot to try and see but if you're in the wrong place you're more likely to make the wrong call…

4 An intentional offence by a defending player in the circle against an opponent who does not have possession of the ball or an opportunity to play the ball.

5 When the ball becomes lodged in a players clothing or equipment while in the circle they are defending.

TIP FOR ASSISTING UMPIRES AT PCs:

We all know that the assisting umpire is responsible for the supervision of the players on the centre line, however, their focus and attention should be more towards their colleagues circle and the penalty corner. Their primary role at this time is to assist their colleague. They need to be attentive. There's a lot to look out for. If the controlling umpire thinks they've missed something, they should promptly look to the assisting umpire for advice and that advice will be a signal…a big clear one! The assisting umpire won't (shouldn't) blow the whistle. While the ball / decision is in the **controlling** umpire's circle, it is they who should blow it and award the penalty or free hit.

TIP There are two particularly difficult things for the controlling umpire to see correctly during a penalty corner. One is the **line that the defenders take** as they rush at the attack. The umpire who has the assisting role should be positioned to see clearly and therefore be available to advise the controlling umpire. If the defender is clearly running into the shot or into the taker without making any attempt to play the ball with their stick, they must be penalised for dangerous play. If the assisting umpire is positioned well into the pitch (towards the centre of the pitch is recommended and over the centre line), they should not only see it but be able to offer the signal with complete credibility immediately the engaged (controlling) umpire asks.

The second area that is proving difficult to recognise is the **blocking** at PCs. It is used by attackers and defenders and if left unchecked can result in some very controversial decisions. The umpires really need to work as a team in this area and focus on where the players position themselves and if they intentionally block out other players. There is some good footage available on the internet to demonstrate this and umpires should be encouraged to research it and develop their understanding.

If a penalty corner is awarded immediately before half-time or full-time, the rules require it to be completed. The details of this rule clearly indicate the circumstances that determine when it is completed. With centralised timing, (i.e. with a technical table), it is expected that players know the rules and will not stop playing if time is indicated. This is consistent with the procedure adopted for indoor hockey. If there is no technical table, it is the umpires who are directly responsible for controlling the time and they will be able to take into account the prolongation of the game.

67

In all instances the umpires, (usually the umpire controlling the penalty corner), is responsible for observing and indicating when the penalty corner has been completed.

When is a penalty corner over?

1 When a goal is scored.

2 When a free-hit is awarded to the defending team.

3 When the ball travels more than 5m outside the circle.

4 When the ball is played over the back-line by an attacker or unintentionally by a defender (i.e. another PC is not awarded).

5 When a defender commits an offence which does not result in another PC.

6 When a penalty stroke is awarded.

7 When a bully is awarded.

Penalty stroke

This is when it gets very, very serious! It's the most theatrical of the set pieces…1 v 1 and 2 umpires to supervise! The time has been stopped and all of the non-involved players are positioned beyond the near 23m line. The controlling umpire needs to manage this well and the assisting umpire should not intervene or assist in this management unless it is absolutely necessary. Being there on the back-line approximately 7 or 8m from the post should be enough.

TIP The number one job for the assisting umpire is to confirm that the ball has wholly crossed the line. Stand still. Stand astride the line and focus in on the line. Don't be distracted. Most of the time it's obvious and easy to tell if the ball has crossed but sometimes it isn't…

A penalty stroke can be awarded for any one of three reasons:

1 An offence by a defender in the circle that prevents the probable scoring of a goal.

2 An intentional offence in the circle by a defender against an opponent who has possession of the ball or an opportunity to play the ball.

3 Persistent early breaking off the back-line by defending players while defending penalty corners.

Back in 2007 a significant change was made to the penalty stroke rule. The requirement for teams to play with a goalkeeper was removed and while initially there was a degree of confusion among some of the players and some reluctance on the part of the coaches, it is now quite common especially in the closing minutes of 'must win games' for a team to play 11 field players on the pitch. But the question is, what happens if a PS is awarded and there's no defending goalkeeper on the pitch?

Can they make a substitution?
Yes they can.
Do they have to make a substitution?
No they don't.

If the team defending the stroke has chosen to play only with field players and not use a substitute goalkeeper to defend the penalty stroke, the defender may use only their stick to make a save.

If the player defending the stroke is a goalkeeper, they must wear protective headgear; if the player defending the stroke is otherwise taking part in the game as a field player, they may wear only a face mask as protective equipment.

TIP If your match is part of a tournament, always read the tournament regulations....sometimes the rule is tinkered with in order to suit the competition e.g. if it's an age group event (U16's or 18's etc.)You need to make sure you can supervise it correctly as an error or misunderstanding could result in you taking the blame and this is particularly undesirable if it leads to an injury.

TIP Time is stopped for a penalty stroke. Do not forget to stop your watch! Time is re-started when the whistle is blown to resume play at the end of the penalty stroke... and don't forget to start your watch! That's where so many umpires forget and then 10 minutes before the end of the game, a player says "how much longer ref?" and you look at your watch and freeze!

The stroke taker used to be restricted to taking only one pace before playing the ball. This is no longer the case. The taker needs only to be within playing distance of the ball and playing distance is defined as an outstretched arm and an outstretched stick. The number of steps they take is immaterial.

The taker mustn't feint or dummy at playing the ball. Neither can they follow up for a re-bound once the stroke has been played. Unlike soccer, re-bounds are not permitted at penalties in hockey! (Note that in international hockey some competitions have penalty shoot-outs and in these, rebounds are permitted.)

TIP Always discuss penalty strokes and your respective responsibilities in your pre-match chat.

TIP Before you re-start the match after a PS, check to see that your colleague is back in position (nearer the other half of the pitch) and essentially, looking at you. It is very embarrassing and potentially problematical if you allow the game to begin while the other umpire is still trekking back!

Personal Penalties

Hockey is measured by many sports as a leader in terms of how it deals with misconduct – particularly on the personal penalties side. In principle what we have is a traffic light system. The green card represents a warning only and it doesn't result in a suspension (except in international or some tournament environments – again…always check the regulations). The yellow card is more serious and it represents a temporary suspension of a minimum of 5 minutes (note in indoor hockey it's less). The red card means permanent suspension from the match. The player has to completely leave the playing area and is usually sent off to the dressing room!

Umpires are being encouraged to use their voices more and do more to keep players on the field. Prevention is better than cure as they say. Use your skills and personalities to develop a rapport with the players. The better your rapport, the easier it is to manage the game and good rapport does reduce the risk of friction or conflict.   Management, management, management…

TIP Umpires shouldn't be shy of using their warning cards. If a card is deserved, a card should be shown and it's important to show the card with confidence. Awarding a card is a very visual thing, everyone is looking at you so don't look smug or give off a message of 'it serves you right'. Stay calm and be neutral and if you feel the need to express yourself, do no more than hold your head to one side as if to say, sorry, but I have no choice.

Chapter 10

REFLECTION AND EVALUATION

All officials, whatever their sport, ought to spend some time reflecting about and evaluating how well they are performing in their work. In this chapter we focus on the skills involved in evaluating your performance in order to improve in the future.

First, you need to consider what you want to improve or work on. Second, how you could best go about developing that area. Self-evaluation is not an easy thing to do, however, it is less difficult if you start by being honest.

Rating your performance

Ask yourself some basic questions such as 'Am I happy with my umpiring?' or 'Could I improve this area of my umpiring?' Make a checklist of the tasks that you do and rate them from 1 – 5; did I plan well, was my preparation good, was my body language balanced and appropriate, are my signals clear and given with confidence, was I calm and in control, were my instructions clearly understood? The first time you do this, you may choose to look at the 'whole performance' but subsequently, you may find it useful to consider particular aspects of the umpiring process and focus **only** on these. Perhaps you already have some realistic goals in mind, so here are some suggestions of what to do next.

Write a diary

This can be done quickly after each game and it can be really useful. It will help you to clarify any areas of concern and perhaps any related incidents that occurred during the match. Try to focus on the 'good' as well as the 'not so good'.

Make a video of yourself

Videoing your umpiring can help to highlight a whole variety of areas of your performance and often during the pace and stress of the game, you are unaware that they need attention or improvement. Why not ask someone to do it for you?

Ask a friend or colleague

Feedback from an observer can work well provided the observer knows what to look for. Ask them to recall what happened; don't ask them to judge it.

Get feedback from the players or coaches

Sometimes we don't need to ask as the players and coaches make their feelings very clear, particularly when they believe we have got it wrong. Occasionally they are absolutely right and this is where we need to avoid being defensive. However, they aren't always right…

Asking a player or coach for honest feedback, good and not so good after your game is often the very best learning opportunity. And that's not just for you, it's for them too.

> **TIP** Think of a recent game when someone gave you negative feedback or comments. Did you react defensively? If so, go back and re-live that moment again. What could you do or say that would be a better response? It is likely that this may happen again but next time you'll be ready.

That's it. You are now fully prepared to go forth and improve! You have considered your current umpiring performance and evaluated it. You have also gathered information to enable you to set further targets or goals and thus continue the process of development.

Good luck with your umpiring. The better you get the more you'll enjoy it.

Never give up on getting better.

Chapter 11

OTHER HELPFUL INFORMATION -

1. SAYING THANK YOU

Very, very rarely do umpires find that they are alone after the game. The players firstly thank each other and shake hands and then they turn to the umpires. It's always interesting to hear the different accounts that umpires give regarding what they do, how they do it and why they do it.

Some head in a direct line for each other and completely 'blank' each player they pass on the way, others deliberately go to the biggest huddle of players and plant themselves amongst them joining in the hand-shaking immediately or at least trying to. Some turn their back immediately the final whistle is blown and walk towards the goalkeeper approaching the players, holding out a hand and saying well played or similar. This action sets up the next as the umpire then walks with the goalie towards the players and is naturally carried into the group rather than feeling uncomfortable standing and waiting.

The confident umpire will make it happen and will always have the courage and the communication skills to walk confidently to the players and **thank them** for the game.

> **TIP** When it comes to that hand shake…don't rush. Recognise that you aren't a priority. The players will usually thank each other first. Smile and look the player in the eye. Mean it when you say thank you or well played.

> **TIP** Hockey is for all of us. We all deserve to enjoy it, be challenged by it and be rewarded by it, but you only get back what you put in. Give it your best shot; reap the rewards and good luck.

2. USE OF VIDEO

Hockey uses video in a similar way to other sports such as cricket, rugby and tennis. (Football is about to join the party!) All have adopted video technology for reviewing referees or umpires decisions at their premier events. The primary purpose is to get the correct and fair outcome and video referral has repeatedly proven itself to be the best tool.

All hockey played at the highest level (world level) uses 'live' video at tournaments. Many of you will have seen it in action at the London Olympic Games in the summer of 2012. Instead of there being just the two umpires on the pitch and a reserve at the technical table, a fourth is involved; namely the video umpire. In cooperation with the television broadcaster they use the existing TV camera coverage, supplemented by in-goal cameras.

The only people who can directly refer decisions to the video umpire are the match umpires. The reserve umpire and the technical officials cannot.

In 2010 a new tournament regulation was trialled in world level events and it has proved to be overwhelmingly successful and supported by all involved. A team video referral option was introduced whereby the team can challenge an umpire about a decision in the 23m area and the umpire calls for a video referral. If the referral is upheld the team is entitled to a further referral. If it is not upheld no further referral is available. It's another big step forward for the sport.

3. INDOOR HOCKEY

Indoor hockey is growing! There are more and more local competitions. Some are 'friendly' games and others are competitive and lead to qualifying for higher leagues or tournaments. Irrespective of this, all are fun. The hockey is fast indoors, the sides of the pitch don't allow the ball to go out of play and the game shifts from one end to the other with remarkable speed.

Wherever possible, the FIH Hockey Rules Committee keep the outdoor and indoor rules the same. However, there are some very distinctive features to the indoor game and these are reflected in its rules.

There are no 23m lines on an indoor pitch. The only lines across the pitch are the back lines and the centre line and, if there is an intentional offence by a defending player in their half of the pitch, the umpire should award a penalty corner. In outdoor hockey this 'cruel penalty' as the players call it, applies only in the 23m areas.

A match comprises of two periods of 20 minutes and a half-time interval of 5 minutes. Concentration time is therefore 40 minutes as opposed to 70 (outdoors)…are you getting interested?

One of the key differences between the two games is that in indoor hockey the players are not permitted to hit the ball, (the ball has to be pushed or flicked). Neither are they allowed to raise it unless shooting at goal. This (the raised ball) is an important difference but one that is often misunderstood and, if it is umpired poorly it can spoil a game.

Umpiring indoor hockey is demanding and although the pitch is much smaller in size than an outdoor pitch, the umpires need to be fit and sharp in their decision-making. There may only be six players (per team) permitted on the pitch at any one time but it's busy!

The key thing is that your outdoor skills are transferable to indoor hockey. Why not give it a try?

4. TOURNAMENT HOCKEY

Being a member of the team of umpires appointed to a tournament should be a) an honour, b) a challenge and c) a great opportunity - to learn more and be coached while meeting new people and having fun.

Most tournaments have a technical team and an umpiring team and each is appointed a leader. The tournament director leads the technical team and the umpires manager leads the umpiring team. Umpires Managers sometimes have coaches appointed alongside them so as to offer the umpires every opportunity to develop and grow as the tournament progresses. The key thing to recognise as an umpire who is new to 'tournament hockey world' is that the more you give, the more you will receive. Being in a team is very different to the standard weekend game of hockey. There will be a tournament briefing and you will be expected to attend it and contribute alongside the other umpires. Consistency will be very high on the agenda...not just you being consistent but everyone applying the same interpretations and penalties across the entire event. Supporting each other, respecting each other and helping each other should be your mantra!

Umpires should go to tournaments expecting and prepared to deliver their very best performances. Appointments are usually made on a daily basis and your performance will always be a big part of the decision-making process determining what your next game will be. One of the best pieces of advice you can be given is to treat every game as your final i.e. make it your best game ever. If you start well your confidence and competence will grow and you should be rewarded with good games.

In all probability after each game you will be offered a chance to talk through your performance with your umpires manager or coach. Contribute to this process; it isn't supposed to be you listening to them, rather both of you discussing areas of your performance that were good and establishing how to strengthen any apparent weaknesses. However, there is little point in discussing the 'not so good' unless between you, you come up with solutions. Talk things through, work it out and decide how best to apply it to achieve the desired change. Sometimes it can be something as simple as positioning or just the need to have a higher level of awareness.

At the end of the tournament you should receive a report representing your performance. This report is written by the umpires manager and is usually 'signed off' by the tournament director and it will include reference to your contribution off of the field as well as on i.e. team membership, participation in social events and leadership qualities.

5. SUMMARY OF THE 2013 RULES CHANGES

The changes introduced by the FIH for 2013 aim to simplify the game without altering its fundamental characteristics. All of the changes are highlighted in the FIH Rules of Hockey and as mentioned at the start of this book, there is no substitute for reading them, and reading them thoroughly.

The FIH Rules of Hockey book is available on-line as well as from national associations and federations. It is published in English and Spanish and a number of countries are doing 'in-house' translations so as to reach all members of the world-wide hockey family.

So what are the changes?

The way a goal is scored is amended; it now includes what is sometimes referred to as an "own goal". That is, a goal can now be scored after the ball is touched in the circle by either an attacker or a **defender**. The detailed text is provided in Rule 8 of the Hockey Rules book. It is described as a "mandatory experimental rule" so that it applies at all levels of hockey but, because it is a significant change, it will be monitored closely. After a period of review, the FIH Rules Committee will decide whether or not it becomes a permanent change to the Rules.

The other notable change permits the ball to be **raised intentionally** but safely directly from a free hit using a push, flick or scoop action. This is essentially an evolution of what is known as the "self-pass" from a free hit. By having the option to raise the ball immediately, opposing players will not have had the opportunity to get closer than five metres; a raised ball should be safer. The resultant changes are to Rules 13.2 d and e.

As a consequence of these changes, Rules 13.2.f and g have been deleted.

Lastly but of less concern to umpires and umpiring, technical changes have been made to the stick specification. The specification has been re-written to make it clearer; the method of measuring the bow or rake has been revised.

National Associations have been given the choice as to when to introduce this change. The England Hockey Board (EHB) will introduce the revised stick rule in September 2013.

Full details are available from the FIH Hockey Rules book.

6. UMPIRES PITCH GRID

The following pages show Pitch Grids designed for the use of umpires. The aim is for the umpire to plot their position in relation to play i.e. if the ball is at point X, the umpire should be at point Y.

The first grid shows an example and in this scenario the play is approaching the umpire, close to the attacking 23 and moving at pace.

Point Y is the engaged umpire and point YA is the assisting umpire. The ball is point X.

Experiment with the grids ideally with other umpires. The aim should be to agree principles e.g. who stands where at penalty corners or at the centre pass.

© Umpires Pitch Grid - www.sportsresources.co.uk

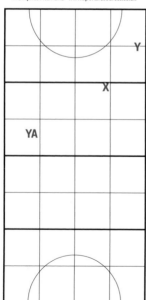

© Umpires Pitch Grid - www.sportsresources.co.uk

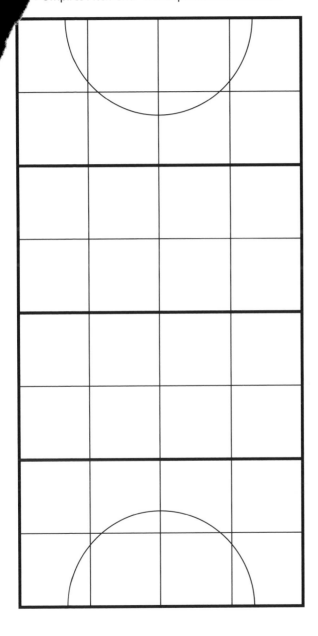

87

© Umpires Pitch Grid - www.sportsresources.co.uk

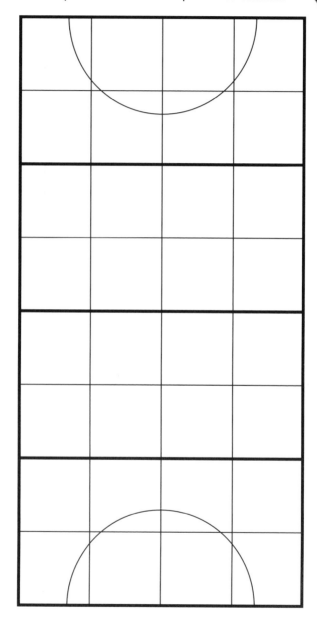

© Umpires Pitch Grid - www.sportsresources.co.uk

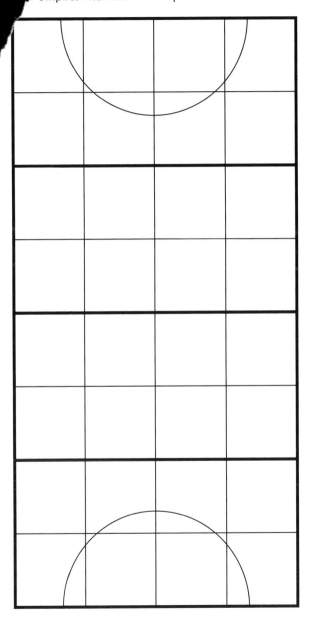

© Umpires Pitch Grid - www.sportsresources.co.uk

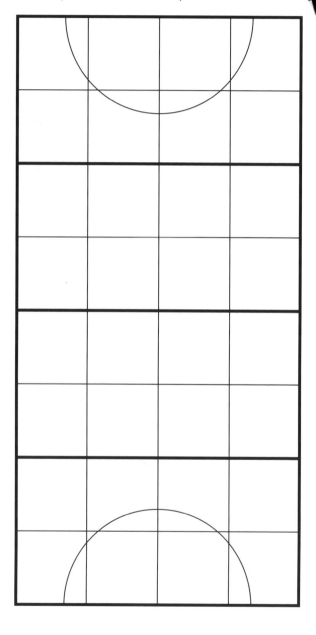

© Umpires Pitch Grid - www.sportsresources.co.uk

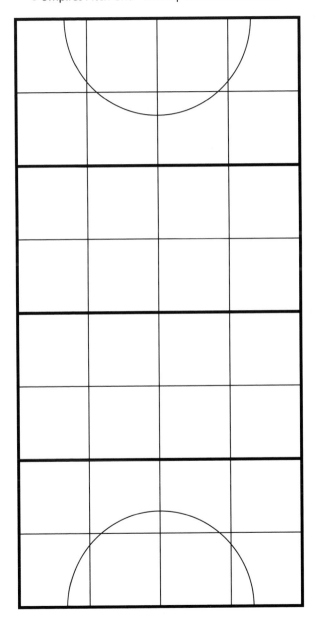

© Umpires Pitch Grid - www.sportsresources.co.uk

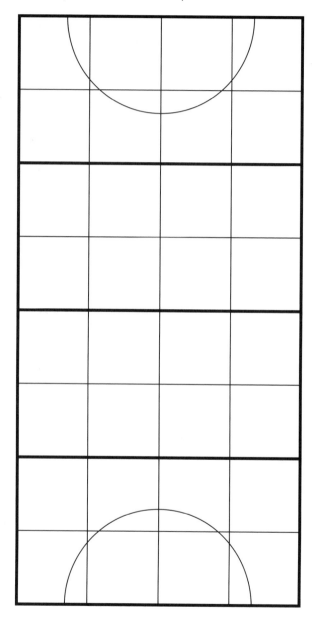

© Umpires Pitch Grid - www.sportsresources.co.uk

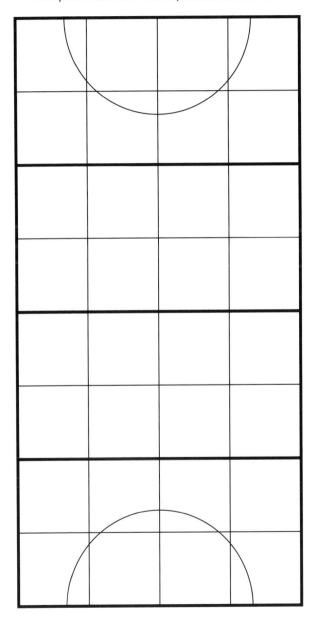

© Umpires Pitch Grid - www.sportsresources.co.uk

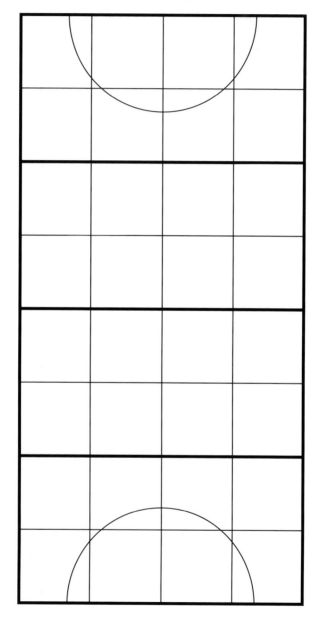

© Umpires Pitch Grid - www.sportsresources.co.uk

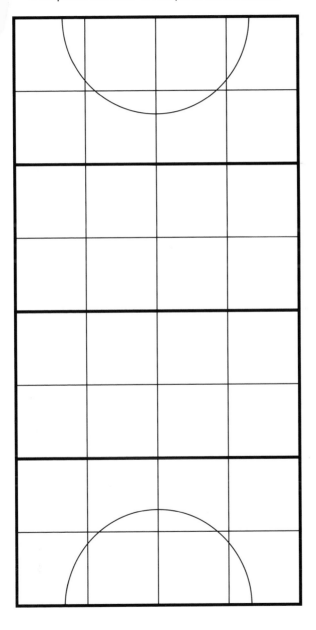

© Umpires Pitch Grid - www.sportsresources.co.uk

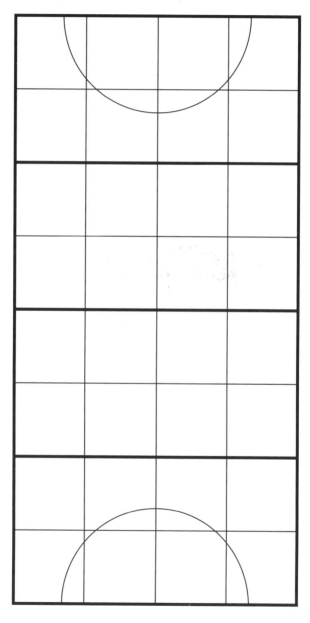